40 Weeks of Prayer for Moms to Be

Requesting God's Comfort, Joy, & Peace

Dr. Latina C. Campbell

Copyright © 2021 Latina C. Campbell

All rights reserved. No part of this book may be reproduced in any form or by any electronic or mechanical means, including information storage and retrieval systems, without permission in writing from the publisher, except by reviewers, who may quote brief passages in a review.

ISBN: 978-1-955312-28-8

Printed in the United States of America

Story Corner Publishing & Consulting, Inc.

1510 Atlanta Ave.

Portsmouth, VA 23704

Storycornerpublishing@yahoo.com

www.StoryCornerPublishing.com

DEDICATION

I give all glory to God for this book because, without Him, there would be no book or me to write it.

I dedicate this book to all the moms-to-be just trying to make it through life. No matter if everyone has turned away, God is still there. He will never leave. Remember, with God, ALL things are possible.

TABLE OF CONTENT

INTRODUCTION

Week 1:	Protection	1
Week 2:	Provision	2
Week 3:	Fighting Depression	3
Week 4:	Feeling Alone	4
Week 5:	Please Send Help	6
Week 6:	Feeling Overwhelmed	7
Week 7:	Feeling Worried & Stressed	9
Week 8:	I Need Direction	11
Week 9:	Afraid	12
Week 10:	Am I Good Enough?	13
Week 11:	Prepare Me, Lord	14
Week 12:	Lord, I Need You to Take Over	15
Week 13:	Save Me from The Cares of Life	17
Week 14:	I Need Peace	20
Week 15:	Give Me Rest	21
Week 16:	Disappointed	22
Week 17:	Discouraged	23
Week 18:	Heal Me, Oh Lord	25
Week 19:	Shower Me with Unspeakable Joy	27
Week 20:	Another Dose of Encouragement	28

TABLE OF CONTENT

Week 21:	Please Pour Strength into Me, Lord	29
Week 22:	I Desire Unconditional Love	30
Week 23:	Confusion & Feeling Lost, Let Me Go!	31
Week 24:	Increase My Patience	32
Week 25:	Feeling Regret	33
Week 26:	Show Me How to Care for Myself Better	34
Week 27:	Help Me to Forgive	35
Week 28:	Keep Me Focus So I Don't Compare	36
Week 29:	No One Understands My Pain	37
Week 30:	Help Me to Prioritize Properly	38
Week 31:	Healthy Baby	39
Week 32:	Impart into Our Baby	40
Week 33:	I Dedicate My Body & Baby Back to You Lord	41
Week 34:	Show Me Our Baby's Purpose	42
Week 35:	Break Generational Curses Off Our Baby	43
Week 36:	Break Soul & Blood Ties Connected to My Baby	44
Week 37:	Prepare My Labor Area Now Lord	45
Week 38:	Please Condition My Partner for Our New Baby	46
Week 39:	Thank You for The Blessing of Life	47
Week 40:	Successful Labor	48

INTRODUCTION

Hi Mama's-to-be,

My many journeys of pregnancy inspired this book. I have been pregnant so many times that I can honestly say each one was a different learning life experience. There was one thing that stayed consistent, and that was my prayer life. I know without a shadow of a doubt now that without prayer, I would not have made it through. My babies would not be here today either. Satan fought me tooth and nail to try and cause miscarriage after miscarriage. I lost two babies to miscarriage because I was so distracted by what I saw going on in my life that I stopped praying. I vowed to myself no more miscarriage no matter how long or how many times I must pray!! Prayer is the ultimate power that God has given us to change things and free ourselves from bondage. Prayer is defined as a solemn request for help or expression of thanks addressed to God.

Prayer is simply a conversation with God. It should be a two-way conversation that grows as your relationship with God grows. Just as you converse with anyone else, speak to God. Then, wait for God to talk back to you. Prayer can be long or short. There is no wrong or right way to pray. If you mean it and believe what you ask, God will respond. He responds with a yes, no, or not yet. When we pray, we must make sure our heart is right. It is essential to always love and forgive so the blessings you pray for will not be delayed.

Jesus (Yeshua in Hebrew) instructed the twelve disciples in the Bible with a guideline on how to pray in scriptures "Matthew 6: 9-13, NIV." As your relationship grows with God, your prayers will shift into a higher dimension.

Guidelines of Prayer:

Matthew 6:5-15 NIV

> "And when you pray, do not be like the hypocrites, for they love to pray standing in the synagogues and on the street corners to be seen by others. Truly I tell you, they have received their reward in full. But when you pray, go into your room, close the door, and pray to your Father, who is unseen. Then your Father, who sees what is done in secret, will reward you. And when you pray, do not keep on babbling like pagans, for they think they will be heard because of their many words. Do not be like them, for your Father knows what you need before you ask him. "This, then, is how you should pray: "Our Father in heaven, hallowed be your name, your kingdom come, your will be done, on earth as it is in heaven. Give us today our daily bread. And forgive us our debts, as we also have forgiven our debtors. And lead us not into temptation but deliver us from the evil one.' For if you forgive other people when they sin against you, your heavenly Father will also forgive you. But if you do not forgive others their sins, your Father will not forgive your sins."

Again, praying with a clean heart makes all the difference when expecting a blessing immediately! How to keep a clean heart? Love & Forgive quickly, freely, and unconditionally. We can not love and forgive just any type of way, but God's way.

God's Love:

1 Corinthians 13:4-8 NIV

> "Love is patient, love is kind. It does not envy, it does not boast, it is not proud. It does not dishonor others, it is not self-seeking, it is not easily angered, it keeps no record of wrongs. Love does not delight in evil but rejoices with the truth. It always protects, always trusts, always hopes, always perseveres.
>
> Love never fails. But where there are prophecies, they will

cease; where there are tongues, they will be stilled; where there is knowledge, it will pass away."

Therefore, live, love, forgive, and pray. There is so much that God has in store for you and your baby. You will get through this pregnancy and joy will be your portion. I love you but know that God loves you best!

- Apostle/ Dr. Latina Campbell

Week 1
PROTECTION

Father, in the name of Jesus,

Thank you, Lord, for being who you are. God, I want to thank you for all that you do for my family and me. God, I come to you today first to ask for forgiveness for anything that I may have done that was not pleasing to you. God, I pray that you would protect my unborn baby and me through this journey of pregnancy. Father, there is a long road ahead for me, but with you, I can make it through. I know there will be many ups and downs, so cover me now. God, I know that you can protect me and my unborn baby beyond what I can do or anyone on this earth. My prayer today is that you would shield me from all hurt, harm, and danger. God, I trust you to be with me for the duration of this pregnancy and beyond. Thank you, in Jesus's name, Amen.

Isaiah 54:17 NIV

> *"no weapon forged against you will prevail, and you will refute every tongue that accuses you. This is the heritage of the servants of the Lord, and this is their vindication from me," declares the Lord."*

- Know that God is the greatest protector.

Week 2
PROVISION

Dear God,

Pregnancy is a significant expense physically, financially, emotionally, and mentally. I know that you are the God who owns everything, including myself and my unborn baby. Therefore, I ask today that you please provide all the necessities that you know we need. God, I thank you for being all-powerful and all-knowing. There is no one like you, no matter how much I tried to compare others to you. You show up when no one else does, and I thank you. You supply when no one else can, and I thank you. God, please help me trust you all the days of my life to provide for my baby and me, in Jesus's name, Amen.

Philippians 4:19 NIV

> *"And my God will meet all your needs according to the riches of his glory in Christ Jesus."*

- If God provided before, He will do it again. Just believe in Him.

Week 3
FIGHTING DEPRESSION

Father God,

There is a fight going on inside of my mind that tires me out every day. I do not want to live like this any longer. Therefore, I come to you for help. I find myself emotional and stressed all the time, and it leads to great depression. I think about the future so much that I fail to realize that I am here in the present living day by day. God, please clear confusion and worry out my mind. Release me from depression because I know it is not normal or healthy for my baby or me. I know so many things want to fight me to miscarry or send me into early labor. Please cover my baby from all complications now. I know that you can step in and block anything. So today, I give all the things that keep me weighed down mentally to you. God, I thank you for the deliverance that I will experience as you encounter me. Please encounter me right now, in Jesus's name, Amen.

Romans 8:28 NIV

> *"And we know that in all things God works for the good of those who love him, who have been called according to his purpose."*

- Depression is Not normal. Know that God is the cure.

Week 4
FEELING ALONE

Dear Lord,

Sometimes I feel as if I'm alone fighting the whole world, and I am exhausted. Lord, I know you are with me every step of the way, but please reveal yourself when I need reassurance. God, please heal me from anything in my past that would push me into thinking I am alone. Please comfort me in my times of need and continue to keep your hands upon my unborn baby. Lord, I thank you for all that you have done thus far. I also thank you for all that you are preparing to do in the life of my baby and me, in Jesus's name, Amen.

Psalm 23 NIV

"The LORD is my shepherd, I lack nothing.
He makes me lie down in green pastures,
he leads me beside quiet waters,
he refreshes my soul.
He guides me along the right paths
for his name's sake.
Even though I walk
through the darkest valley,
I will fear no evil,
for you are with me;
your rod and your staff,
they comfort me.

You prepare a table before me
in the presence of my enemies.
You anoint my head with oil;

my cup overflows.
Surely your goodness and love will follow me
all the days of my life,
and I will dwell in the house of the Lord
forever."

- Remember God is spirit, and He is always everywhere.

Week 5
PLEASE SEND HELP

God,

Thank you for always keeping me in mind even when I don't keep you in mind. I thank you for having plans of good for me and not of evil. God, I end up with the short end of the stick a lot of times. I find myself pouring out to everyone and have nothing left for myself. At times I need help, but I have no one to turn to in those moments. Father, I pull on you today because I know that you are a helper when needed. I need your help so I can make it through another day. You know what areas I need help in; therefore, I invite you in, Lord. Please help me to get through this pregnancy in my right mind and not depleted. I know that you can do all things, and I trust you, in Jesus's name, Amen.

Hebrews 13:6 NIV

> *"So we say with confidence, "The Lord is my helper; I will not be afraid. What can mere mortals do to me?"*

- God helps those in need. Take your superhero cape off and allow Him to step into your situation.

Week 6
FEELING OVERWHELMED

Father,

I come to you today to release all the things that burden me. I have taken on so many things that I have found myself overwhelmed. I have to be superwoman for so many, but no one understands all I go through. I know I could never match up to you when it comes to helping others, so I ask you to help me to know when I should say "no." I need a refill of strength today. I thank you for the people that do help me from time to time, but only you know exactly what I need and when I need it. I thank you for being all that you are in my life. God, I pray that you would relieve me from everything that overwhelms me day to day. I do not want to worry about a "To-Do List" so much that it keeps me from receiving proper sleep. I lay all my concerns at your feet today, in Jesus's name, Amen.

Psalm 90 NIV

> "Lord, you have been our dwelling place
> throughout all generations.
> Before the mountains were born
> or you brought forth the whole world,
> from everlasting to everlasting you are God.
>
> You turn people back to dust,
> saying, "Return to dust, you mortals."
> A thousand years in your sight
> are like a day that has just gone by,
> or like a watch in the night.
> Yet you sweep people away in the sleep of death—

they are like the new grass of the morning:
In the morning it springs up new,
but by evening it is dry and withered.

We are consumed by your anger
and terrified by your indignation.
You have set our iniquities before you,
our secret sins in the light of your presence.
All our days pass away under your wrath;
we finish our years with a moan.
Our days may come to seventy years,
or eighty, if our strength endures;
yet the best of them are but trouble and sorrow,
for they quickly pass, and we fly away.
If only we knew the power of your anger!
Your wrath is as great as the fear that is your due.
Teach us to number our days,
that we may gain a heart of wisdom.

Relent, Lord! How long will it be?
Have compassion on your servants.
Satisfy us in the morning with your unfailing love,
that we may sing for joy and be glad all our days.
Make us glad for as many days as you have afflicted us,
for as many years as we have seen trouble.
May your deeds be shown to your servants,
your splendor to their children.

May the favor of the Lord our God rest on us;
establish the work of our hands for us—
yes, establish the work of our hands."

- It is okay to take a break for yourself and say "no" to others.

Week 7
FEELING WORRIED & STRESSED

Lord,

I thank you for being you. I don't have to have all the strength and answers in the world because you are with me. You are mighty and strong. Being pregnant has welcomed more thoughts in my mind than usual. I find myself trying to deal with them all but continue to come up short. I only want the best for my baby, so please show me how to achieve that. I do not want to stress about having enough finances, who would look after my baby when I start working if I would be a good enough mother once my baby is born, etc. God, I know your spirit is here to comfort and guide us; therefore, please take over. I pray that your Holy Spirit leads me through the worry and stress that piles up in my life. I need comfort and guidance today, oh Lord. Please hear my cry and strip me of the thoughts that plagued me. Help me to trust that you will be there for all my needs and my baby's needs. Lord, please have your way in my life right now, in Jesus's name, Amen.

Matthew 6:19-34 NIV

> *"Do not store up for yourselves treasures on earth, where moths and vermin destroy, and where thieves break in and steal. But store up for yourselves treasures in heaven, where moths and vermin do not destroy, and where thieves do not break in and steal. For where your treasure is, there your heart will be also. The eye is the lamp of the body. If your eyes are healthy, your whole body will be full of light. But if your eyes are unhealthy, your whole body will be full of darkness. If then*

the light within you is darkness, how great is that darkness! No one can serve two masters.

Either you will hate the one and love the other, or you will be devoted to the one and despise the other. You cannot serve both God and money. Therefore, I tell you, do not worry about your life, what you will eat or drink; or about your body, what you will wear. Is not life more than food, and the body more than clothes?

Look at the birds of the air; they do not sow or reap or store away in barns, and yet your heavenly Father feeds them. Are you not much more valuable than they? Can any one of you by worrying add a single hour to your life? And why do you worry about clothes? See how the flowers of the field grow. They do not labor or spin. Yet I tell you that not even Solomon in all his splendor was dressed like one of these. If that is how God clothes the grass of the field, which is here today and tomorrow is thrown into the fire, will he not much more clothe you—you of little faith?

So do not worry, saying, 'What shall we eat?' or 'What shall we drink?' or 'What shall we wear?' For the pagans run after all these things, and your heavenly Father knows that you need them. But seek first his kingdom and his righteousness, and all these things will be given to you as well. Therefore, do not worry about tomorrow, for tomorrow will worry about itself. Each day has enough trouble of its own."

- God knows best because He created all things, including you and me. He knows what we will go through before we go through it because He is all-knowing. So, give God the things that worry you.

Week 8
I NEED DIRECTION

Father God,

I have been going in circles, and it's frustrating. I know that you know the way, so please show me. I come to you in need of your direction for my life because I do not want to go through any more delay. I have lost sight of the way and have become distracted with the cares of life. Please help me to understand what this week should consist of and what my purpose is in it. God, I pray that as this week goes by, I fulfill the assignments you give me. Thank you for my purpose. Please remind me of my purpose and keep me on track when I become distracted; in Jesus's name, Amen.

Proverbs 3:6 NIV

> *"in all your ways submit to him, and he will make your paths straight."*

- Jesus is the way, the truth, and the life. Therefore, seek Him direction.

Week 9
AFRAID

God,

Thank you for caring for my baby and me. I know that you are with us and want the best for us. Somehow, I have become afraid of the future this week. So many things have magnified themselves in my life. The unknown is one of them. You know each situation that has come my way, and I pray that you help me not to be afraid to continue with the journey of pregnancy. I know each battle I face belongs to you, so God, please help me to turn them over to you as they come. I really need your help today, in Jesus's name, Amen.

Isaiah 41:10 NIV

> *"So do not fear, for I am with you; do not be dismayed, for I am your God. I will strengthen you and help you; I will uphold you with my righteous right hand."*

- God does not give us fear. He gives us His power, love, and a sound mind to get through life.

Week 10
AM I GOOD ENOUGH ?

Lord Jesus,

This week I am struggling with the thoughts of being a good enough mother. I know being a mother is a lot of work. God, I ask that you please prepare me for everything I must do and become for my unborn child. Help me to be enough and not fail at providing what my baby needs. God, I thank you for being a father to me and showing me what enough looks like and is. I pray that as I walk through motherhood, I bring you glory each day, in Jesus's name, Amen.

Ephesians 2:10 NIV

> "For we are God's handiwork, created in Christ Jesus to do good works, which God prepared in advance for us to do."

- If God thought you were not good enough, He would have never called you to it.

Week 11
PREPARE ME, LORD

Dear God,

Thank you for the gift of life. Thank you for the blessing of being able to birth a new baby. God, it takes a lot to raise a baby and prepare to bring a new life into my family, so please position me to be ready. I pray that not only do you help me to get prepared, but I pray that you help my partner to prepare as well for parenthood. Father, I pray that upon the arrival of our new baby that everything will be in place, and I don't have to worry about anything last minute. I pray that you give me the wisdom to have everything prepared and not overwhelm myself with the things that do not matter. Lord, I pray that everything will flow smoothly and there will be no friction in, Jesus's name, Amen.

1 Corinthians 16:13 NIV

> *"Be on your guard; stand firm in the faith; be courageous; be strong."*

- God placed everything you need inside of you. Stop focusing so much on the things. Everything will happen how it needs to if you allow God to be in control.

Week 12
LORD, I NEED YOU TO TAKE OVER

Dear Lord,

I am not sure what is going on this week, but I feel low and cannot get myself together. People say depression is huge in pregnancy, and I am not sure if this is bringing me low. If things were in order and I had the help I needed, depression or stress would not play a part in my pregnancy. Lord, I need you to step in today to ensure my whole week does not go this way. Please put everything in place so depression or stress does not overtake me. I desire to have joy and peace in my pregnancy and life. God, please help me see the brighter side of life, and please change my perspective when it is off. Please touch the hearts of the people in my life so that they do not add to the stress of pregnancy from today forward. Please cover my baby so that stress does not attack its growth. Settle my mind, and please shower me with love today, in Jesus's name, Amen.

Psalm 139:1-18 NIV

>"You have searched me, Lord,
> and you know me.
> You know when I sit and when I rise;
> you perceive my thoughts from afar.
> You discern my going out and my lying down;
> you are familiar with all my ways.
> Before a word is on my tongue
> you, Lord, know it completely.
> You hem me in behind and before,
> and you lay your hand upon me.

Such knowledge is too wonderful for me,
too lofty for me to attain.

Where can I go from your Spirit?
Where can I flee from your presence?
If I go up to the heavens, you are there;
if I make my bed in the depths, you are there.
If I rise on the wings of the dawn,
if I settle on the far side of the sea,
even there your hand will guide me,
your right hand will hold me fast.
If I say, "Surely the darkness will hide me
and the light become night around me,"
even the darkness will not be dark to you;
the night will shine like the day,
for darkness is as light to you.

For you created my inmost being;
you knit me together in my mother's womb.
I praise you because I am fearfully and wonderfully made;
your works are wonderful,
I know that full well.
My frame was not hidden from you
when I was made in the secret place,
when I was woven together in the depths of the earth.
Your eyes saw my unformed body;
all the days ordained for me were written in your book
before one of them came to be.
How precious to me are your thoughts, God!
How vast is the sum of them!
Were I to count them,
they would outnumber the grains of sand—
when I awake, I am still with you."

- Do not claim depression because it is not normal to hold. Depression happens but release It to God so you can see things clearly.

Week 13
SAVE ME FROM THE CARES OF LIFE

Father God,

I thank you for all that you are. I thank you for my life and my unborn baby. Lord, please strip me from all things that are not of you. Please save me from all the cares of life where I become stuck. Lord, I get so overwhelmed when focusing on so many things that I become drained. Exhaustion hit me, and I want to lay down and sleep the day away or take a nap to reset and start over again. I know life is supposed to happen with many ups and downs, but please help me to go with your flow for my life. God, please cover and protect my unborn baby so that I shall not have a miscarriage from stress or go into premature labor, and my baby is born unhealthy. Lord, help me to be the best version of me so I can be what I need to be for my baby, in Jesus's name, Amen.

Psalm 27 NIV

> *"The Lord is my light and my salvation—*
> *whom shall I fear?*
> *The Lord is the stronghold of my life—*
> *of whom shall I be afraid?*
>
> *When the wicked advance against me*
> *to devour me,*
> *it is my enemies and my foes*
> *who will stumble and fall.*
>
> *Though an army besiege me,*
> *my heart will not fear;*

*though war break out against me,
even then I will be confident.*

*One thing I ask from the Lord,
this only do I seek:
that I may dwell in the house of the Lord
all the days of my life,
to gaze on the beauty of the Lord
and to seek him in his temple.
For in the day of trouble
he will keep me safe in his dwelling;
he will hide me in the shelter of his sacred tent
and set me high upon a rock.*

*Then my head will be exalted
above the enemies who surround me;
at his sacred tent I will sacrifice with shouts of joy;
I will sing and make music to the Lord.*

*Hear my voice when I call, Lord;
be merciful to me and answer me.
My heart says of you, "Seek his face!"
Your face, Lord, I will seek.
Do not hide your face from me,
do not turn your servant away in anger;
you have been my helper.
Do not reject me or forsake me,
God my Savior.
Though my father and mother forsake me,
the Lord will receive me.
Teach me your way, Lord;
lead me in a straight path
because of my oppressors.
Do not turn me over to the desire of my foes,
for false witnesses rise up against me,
spouting malicious accusations.*

I remain confident of this:

I will see the goodness of the Lord
in the land of the living.
Wait for the Lord;
be strong and take heart
and wait for the Lord."

-We all go through tough things, but do not get stuck there! You need to pass the test and move on with life.

Week 14
I NEED PEACE

Lord,

Sometimes I have peace, and other times I feel as if it's stolen. I pray that you released peace unto me for this week so that I shall not be shaken with things that are thrown my way. God, I know that you are peace, so I ask you to overflow in my life today like never before. I thank you for hearing my cry and prayer today. I even thank you in advance for the peace that shall overtake my body for this week, in Jesus's name, Amen.

Philippians 4:6-8 NIV

> *"Do not be anxious about anything, but in every situation, by prayer and petition, with thanksgiving, present your requests to God. And the peace of God, which transcends all understanding, will guard your hearts and your minds in Christ Jesus. Finally, brothers and sisters, whatever is true, whatever is noble, whatever is right, whatever is pure, whatever is lovely, whatever is admirable—if anything is excellent or praiseworthy—think about such things."*

- God is in control of all things. Therefore, seek God for the answers you desire.

Week 15
GIVE ME REST

Father,

I thank you for being powerful and perfect. I thank you for being all that you are to me. I pull on you today for rest, Lord. Please show me when I need to rest and when I should be working. Lord, help me to be balanced in everything I do. Today I feel overworked and needing a break, but there is still so much to be done. My unborn baby is coming soon, and I pray that everything gets done before the baby arrives. Help me not to be exhausted and miss the moment to enjoy my baby's arrival, in Jesus's name, Amen.

Matthew 11:28-30 NIV

> *"Come to me, all you who are weary and burdened, and I will give you rest. Take my yoke upon you and learn from me, for I am gentle and humble in heart, and you will find rest for your souls. For my yoke is easy and my burden is light."*

- It is ok to take it easy. Put your pride aside and ask others for help when it gets to be too much for you.

Week 16
DISAPPOINTED

God,

Thank you for your perfect will. I worship you because you are perfect. You created all things, including my unborn baby and me; thank you. Please help me to understand your will for my life so that I may not be disappointed ever again by following my own will. Many things run through my mind that I feel should go a certain way, but because they don't, I have been disappointed repeatedly. Today I asked you to reshape my perspective regarding people, places, and things. I even ask that you show me who I am supposed to be, what I should be doing, and where I am supposed to be in life. Disappointment hurts, and I am tired of experience it. Therefore, please take away the pain and please heal me, father. I thank you for the plans that you have for my life because I know they're good and not evil. Please reveal your goals so that I will not be tossed from left to right with my plans anymore, in Jesus's name, Amen.

1 Peter 4:8 NIV

> "Above all, love each other deeply, because love covers over a multitude of sins."

- People may disappoint us, or we may even do it to ourselves, but love keeps no record of wrongs. Forgive yourself and others, then seek God on which way to go next. God does know best because He is an all-knowing God.

Week 17
DISCOURAGED

Lord Jesus,

I am not sure how I got to this place, but I feel discouraged. Pregnancy should be a joy, but I tend to focus on the things that I do not have yet, and it discourages me. Lord, I do not have anyone in my life that motivates me or pushes me when I get stuck in these dark places. I pray you will overflow in my life and send your encouragement. I need you to survive, Lord. I am learning that every single day. Pregnancy wears a lot on me, and I pray that I could experience the joy in it from this day forward, in Jesus's name, Amen.

Psalm 34 NIV

> "I will extol the Lord at all times;
> his praise will always be on my lips.
> I will glory in the Lord;
> let the afflicted hear and rejoice.
> Glorify the Lord with me;
> let us exalt his name together.
>
> I sought the Lord, and he answered me;
> he delivered me from all my fears.
> Those who look to him are radiant;
> their faces are never covered with shame.
> This poor man called, and the Lord heard him;
> he saved him out of all his troubles.
> The angel of the Lord encamps around those who fear him,
> and he delivers them.

Taste and see that the Lord is good;
blessed is the one who takes refuge in him.
Fear the Lord, you his holy people,
for those who fear him lack nothing.
The lions may grow weak and hungry,
but those who seek the Lord lack no good thing.
Come, my children, listen to me;
I will teach you the fear of the Lord.
Whoever of you loves life
and desires to see many good days,
keep your tongue from evil
and your lips from telling lies.
Turn from evil and do good;
seek peace and pursue it.

The eyes of the Lord are on the righteous,
and his ears are attentive to their cry;
but the face of the Lord is against those who do evil,
to blot out their name from the earth.

The righteous cry out, and the Lord hears them;
he delivers them from all their troubles.
The Lord is close to the brokenhearted
and saves those who are crushed in spirit.

The righteous person may have many troubles,
but the Lord delivers him from them all;
he protects all his bones,
not one of them will be broken.

Evil will slay the wicked;
the foes of the righteous will be condemned.

The Lord will rescue his servants;
no one who takes refuge in him will be condemned."

- Satan wants us to give up when we are on the right track. Do not allow him to fool you. If you are doing what you are supposed to be doing, don't stop! Keep going until you see results.

Week 18
HEAL ME, OH LORD

Dear God,

I thank you for sharing being The Healer that knows best for my body. I lay my body on the altar today and request your healing because I do not feel normal. My body is stiff with many aches and pains that were not there before. I can hardly breathe at times, and it's becoming hard to walk. You have helped so many others; therefore, I believe you for my healing. I pray your report will prevail no matter what the doctors say, or I think sometimes. I also pray you cover and protect my unborn baby through my healing process. If my baby needs healing too, I pray that you do it for the baby as well, in Jesus's name, Amen.

Psalm 41NIV

"Blessed are those who have regard for the weak;
the Lord delivers them in times of trouble.
The Lord protects and preserves them—
they are counted among the blessed in the land—
he does not give them over to the desire of their foes.
The Lord sustains them on their sickbed
and restores them from their bed of illness.

I said, "Have mercy on me, Lord;
heal me, for I have sinned against you."
My enemies say of me in malice,
"When will he die and his name perish?"
When one of them comes to see me,
he speaks falsely, while his heart gathers slander;

then he goes out and spreads it around.

All my enemies whisper together against me;
they imagine the worst for me, saying,
"A vile disease has afflicted him;
he will never get up from the place where he lies."

Even my close friend,
someone I trusted,
one who shared my bread,
has turned against me.

But may you have mercy on me, Lord;
raise me up, that I may repay them.
I know that you are pleased with me,
for my enemy does not triumph over me.
Because of my integrity you uphold me
and set me in your presence forever.

Praise be to the Lord, the God of Israel,
from everlasting to everlasting.
Amen and Amen."

- When we trust God, there is no limit to what He can bring us through in our life.

Week 19
SHOWER ME WITH UNSPEAKABLE JOY

God,

I thank you for waking me up today and allowing me to carry a healthy baby. The responsibility that weighs on my shoulders every day makes me feel as if there is no time for me. Help me to practice self-care and to do just as much for myself as I do for others. Lord, shine the light on what kills my joy, and please release me from it right now, in Jesus's name, Amen.

Romans 15:13 NIV

> *"May the God of hope fill you with all joy and peace as you trust in him, so that you may overflow with hope by the power of the Holy Spirit."*

- Schedule self-care routines just as you would schedule a doctor's appointment. Put it on your schedule and stick to it no matter what happens.

Week 20
ANOTHER DOSE OF ENCOURAGEMENT

Lord,

I have gained some extra weight, my hair has thinned out, my feet are swollen, and I cannot move as I have in the past. I wonder if I am still attractive to my partner because I feel I am not. I have thoughts that no one wants me anymore, not even myself. I want to feel sexy again and to remember that pregnancy is beautiful also! This extra weight has made me unhappy. I know my body must change for the baby, but I miss my perfect curves and shape. I may not have been in the complete figure I wanted to be before getting pregnant, but I had a better chance of working towards that goal. Now all I do is look at myself in the mirror, getting bigger and having a more challenging time managing getting around. I know my partner enjoys the visual aspect of life, and I pray he does not look at me in disgust because I do not look the same. Please encourage me to look at myself how you see me, in Jesus's name, Amen.

Song of Songs 4:7 NIV

> "You are altogether beautiful, my darling; there is no flaw in you."

- No matter what we look like, we are all special to God. He created us perfectly in His image. He loves us unconditionally, no matter what others think.

Week 21
PLEASE POUR STRENGTH INTO ME, LORD

Father God,

I feel so exhausted every day. I know I am carrying another life inside of me, and I thank you for my baby. Please pour your strength back into me as my baby and others pull on me. I find myself just wanting to sleep, but I have so many things to do. I am not sure if I have too many things to do or if I do not have enough strength to do what I must. Please guide me through my schedule and strengthen me so I do not feel so drained all the time; in Jesus's name, Amen.

Joshua 1:9 NIV

> "Have I not commanded you? Be strong and courageous. Do not be afraid; do not be discouraged, for the Lord your God will be with you wherever you go."

- Be realistic with your schedule. We are not superwoman, and it is ok to take a break for yourself.

Week 22
DESIRE UNCONDITIONAL LOVE

God,

I thank you for waking me up today. I have another chance to see something I have never seen. I know you are with me because most of the things I go through I could not have gotten through alone. Lord, sometimes when I go through things, I find myself feeling unloved. When I do get love, it comes with a price or has stipulations attached. That leads me to question if it is even love in the first place. God, please show me what real unconditional love is so that I can give it to my unborn baby. Send people into my life that will love my baby and me unconditionally as well. I thank you in advance, in Jesus's name, Amen.

John 3:16 NIV

> "For God so loved the world that he gave his one and only Son, that whoever believes in him shall not perish but have eternal life."

- We get what we give out. Make sure you are always giving God's love out so you can spot God's love in return. If others are not giving you God's love, you do not have to receive it. You have choices in life.

Week 23
CONFUSION & FEELING LOST, LET ME GO!

Lord,

Today I am not feeling my best. I know I can call on you to correct whatever is going on. I am grateful to have a God like you. No one can compare to you. I have moments that I feel lost and confused. I move a step forward, but it seems I am going backward when it comes to results. Please reveal to me if I am doing something wrong. I no longer want to feel lost. Please clear my mind and help me to focus on you, in Jesus's name, Amen.

2 Timothy 2:7 NIV

> *"Reflect on what I am saying, for the Lord will give you insight into all this."*

- Allow God to lead your every step. We may have plans that seem good, but God's plans and ways are always right. There is a big difference between good and right.

Week 24
INCREASE MY PATIENCE

Lord Jesus,

I thank you for your love, mercy, and grace towards me. I know it takes patience to deal with me, and I am thankful that you extend it to me. Please help me to increase my tolerance in dealing with others and the situations in my life. I know I will need the patience to be a mother, so please work on me now. I thank you in advance, in Jesus's name, Amen.

Ecclesiastes 7:8 NIV

> "The end of a matter is better than its beginning, and patience is better than pride."

- Patience is a characteristic of God that we need to follow. Our character should be identical to His. Therefore, patience is not an option. It is mandatory.

Week 25
FEELING REGRET

Father in Heaven,

Thank you, God, for all that you have done in my life. I know I could not have done any of it without you. This pregnancy, for example, is one of them. Lord, I am dealing with regret today because things are not going the way I planned them to go. I know my ways are not your ways, and my plans are not your plans, but Lord, I feel as if this pregnancy is all a mistake sometimes. Everyone said I should have waited, I should not have made this baby with the person I did, or that I should not have had this baby at all. Sometimes I hear what they say even when I am not in their presence, and I wonder if it is all true. Ever since I found out I was pregnant, things have gotten tough for me. I have moments of regret, but I am thankful to carry a baby at all because some women cannot. Lord, help me to see things your way and to go with whatever you desire of my life, in Jesus's name, Amen.

John 14:1 NIV

> "Let not your hearts be troubled. Believe in God; believe also in me."

- Children are blessings from God no matter how they came about. If God did not want the child to be born, it would not happen. God has the final say in all things because He is sovereign and is in control of everything.

Week 26
SHOW ME HOW TO CARE FOR MYSELF BETTER

Heavenly Father,

I have so much to do daily, but I know I need to plan time for myself. Lord, help me make time for myself first, so I am not exhausted when it's my turn. Please show me how to care for myself better without feeling guilty. Everyone in my circle looks up to me for strength and care for them, but no one extends that same helping hand back to me. God, please show me how to value myself even when no one else does. I know I suppose to love everyone, but please help me not to forget to love myself first, in Jesus's name, Amen.

Ephesians 5:29 NIV

> "After all, no one ever hated their own body, but they feed and care for their body, just as Christ does the church—"

- God wants us to love others as we love ourselves. That implies our love comes first in order to give others from the overflow.

Week 27
HELP ME TO FORGIVE

God,

I go through so much, and sometimes I do not know how to process it all. Lord, I thank you for being so forgiving when I mess up. Please help me to forgive others when they do me wrong. Please show me how to handle people and not take them so seriously that what they do becomes personal. I do not like to be hurt or even cry. Therefore, please change my perspective about the trials I face. Reveal the people for who they are so that I do not surround myself with those, not in my best interest. Please help me to release the people to you who have hurt me, in Jesus's name, Amen.

Colossians 3:12-13 NIV

> "Therefore, as God's chosen people, holy and dearly loved, clothe yourselves with compassion, kindness, humility, gentleness and patience. Bear with each other and forgive one another if any of you has a grievance against someone. Forgive as the Lord forgave you."

- Forgiveness is not for the people. It is for you to move on. If you do not forgive others, God will place you in holding until you forgive. Once you forgive, God deals with the people accordingly. Forgive them, for they know not what they entirely do.

Week 28
KEEP ME FOCUS SO I DON'T COMPARE

Lord,

Thank you for this day and my unborn baby. I know I should be happy 24/7, but I tend to look at other people's lives and feel I should be so much further. Pregnancy has put me in panic mode because I want to be the best for my child and myself. The weeks are going by so fast, and I want to have everything set in place before the baby comes. I know what is for me will be but help me not compare my life and process to anyone else. Please show me where you want me to be and help me to get there. I want to be satisfied with your will for my life. God, I give you my mind and heart to deal with this matter, in Jesus's name, Amen.

Ephesians 2:10 NIV

> "For we are God's handiwork, created in Christ Jesus to do good works, which God prepared in advance for us to do."

- Whatever God assigned to your life is just as good as the next person's life. God has plans for us all to prosper, which does not mean it will all look the same. Be ok with your differences because there is only one you.

Week 29
NO ONE UNDERSTANDS MY PAIN

God,

Thank you for being so understanding in all situations of my life, even when no one else does. I pray that people in my life will be more understanding of what I go through each day. I know I am the one that is pregnant and is experiencing pain firsthand. I feel pain in my body, mind, and even emotions sometimes, but please help me to be patient with those who will not understand. Lord, please heal me and send helpers my way to encourage me through this journey of pregnancy, in Jesus's name, Amen.

Psalm 147:3 NIV

> "He heals the brokenhearted and binds up their wounds."

- The truth is no one is going to understand what you go through in detail except God because He knows all things. Do not fault the people for their lack of understanding. If God does not open their minds to it, then it simply will not be. Take all matters to God and pray for healing.

Week 30
HELP ME TO PRIORITIZE PROPERLY

Lord,

Since I have been pregnant, my schedule has been all over the place. I know I have added a lot to my "To-Do List" on top of countless doctor appointments, but please help me filter through it all. Please show me how to prioritize what is essential and take away what is not needed. My mind is constantly racing in a panic to ensure I have done everything before my baby arrives. I know I can overreact concerning planning as well. Help me not to become burnt out before my baby comes, in Jesus's name, Amen.

Matthew 6:33 NIV

> *"But seek first the kingdom of God and his righteousness, and all these things will be added to you."*

- Now is the time only to do what is necessary. Rest is for these weeks to come because you will need it.

Week 31
HEALTHY BABY

Father God,

I pray that you cover and protect my unborn baby through these weeks remaining. It has been a long process, but we are approaching the end of the journey now. God, I could not have gotten this far without you, and I thank you. I pray that my baby is healthy and does not need to stay in the hospital for any reason after I am discharged. Please assign the doctors that will be in the room during the time of delivery and the nurses who will care for my baby during our stay. Please send your spirit to the room where my baby will be born, and we will sleep right now, in Jesus's name, Amen.

Galatians 3:26 ESV

"For in Christ Jesus you are all sons of God, through faith."

- God is in control of all things. Therefore, trust Him to protect your baby.

Week 32
IMPART INTO OUR BABY

Father, in the name of Jesus,

Thank you for my unborn baby. I pray that you impart your Word into my baby right now, and it will not go astray in life. I pray that you will enter my womb and encounter my baby today. I pray that when my baby is born that it will know you without a doubt. I pray your spirit will rest in and rule upon my baby's life, in Jesus's name, Amen.

Galatians 4:6 ESV

> "And because you are sons, God has sent the Spirit of his Son into our hearts, crying, "Abba! Father!"

- Allow God to take over your baby's life because He will be there even when you can't. We want the best for our children, but the best is God.

Week 33
I DEDICATE MY BODY & BABY BACK TO YOU LORD

Lord, Jesus,

I have been to many places and done so many things, but now I want to put you first. I know you value your creation which is myself and my baby. Therefore, I want to dedicate my body and my baby to you. I lay myself down on the altar today as a sacrifice to you. I dedicate my baby to you so you can have your way in its life. I trust you because you know best so, please have your way with my baby and me. I surrender us both to you because I know we are in good hands. You have shown me time and time again that you love me unconditionally, and I thank you. Lord, have your way, in Jesus's name, Amen.

1 Corinthians 6: 19-20 ESV

> *"Or do you not know that your body is a temple of the Holy Spirit within you, whom you have from God? You are not your own, for you were bought with a price. So, glorify God in your body."*

- God has a plan for us all. Welcome Him in to show you what that is and walk in it. You will not be disappointed.

Week 34
SHOW ME OUR BABY'S PURPOSE

Father God,

My baby will be here soon, and I am so excited! I am a little nervous also. Therefore, I pray that you will guide me through motherhood. Lord, you have given me a baby to raise, and I am grateful. I do not want to disappoint you because I know my baby is a gift that did not have to happen, but it did. Please show me what the purpose is of this child. I want to help it grow towards what you desire for its life. I thank you for the opportunity to mother a baby of my own, in Jesus's name, Amen.

Matthew 28:18-20 NIV

> "Then Jesus came to them and said, "All authority in heaven and on earth has been given to me. Therefore go and make disciples of all nations, baptizing them in the name of the Father and of the Son and of the Holy Spirit, and teaching them to obey everything I have commanded you. And surely I am with you always, to the very end of the age."

- We produce children to become disciples of Jesus Christ, not just to fill the earth and take up space. Train your child in the ways of Jesus so that they can teach others.

Week 35
BREAK GENERATIONAL CURSES OFF OUR BABY

God,

I thank you for always protecting me even when I did not know you were there. I pray that you protect my baby as well. Lord, I know my bloodline has done so many things that were not pleasing to you. I pray that you forgive them, for they do not know what they do. Please forgive me also for all my sins. I pray that you break every generational curse in my family and that my baby will not be affected. I pray that the curse ends with me. Please allow my child to have a clean slate from this day forward, in Jesus's name, Amen.

Galatians 3:13 NIV

> "Christ redeemed us from the curse of the law by becoming a curse for us—for it is written, "Cursed is everyone who is hanged on a tree."

- The sins of our fathers follow us if we do not ask for forgiveness on their behalf. The same applies if we sin. It will fall on our children if we do not ask for forgiveness.

Week 36
BREAK SOUL & BLOOD TIES CONNECTED TO MY BABY

Lord,

Thank you for dying for the sins of the world. Thank you for your blood that washes us clean. I pray by the power of your blood that every strange authority ruling in my life and destiny is broken and destroyed. I command every power remotely controlling my affections, lose your hold and die! Lord, I pray that you forgive me for connecting to people that I should not have. Destroy those connections to my child now, in Jesus's name, Amen.

1 John 1:9 NIV

> "If we confess our sins, he is faithful and just to forgive us our sins and to cleanse us from all unrighteousness."

- Make sure you ask God to break all connections of the past because they have a way of following us. Leave the past in the past and always pray for your child.

Week 37
PREPARE MY LABOR AREA NOW LORD

Heavenly Father,

Thank you for getting me to the last weeks of pregnancy. Some weeks I wanted to give up, but you were there pushing me through. It is almost that time to bring forth my baby, and I am so excited. God, I pray that you go before my baby and me and prepare the space for us. Please purify the hospital with your fire and send your Holy Spirit to reside there right now. God, please place your angels in our room and surround the entire hospital in Jesus's name, Amen.

Deuteronomy 31:8 NIV

> *"The LORD himself goes before you and will be with you; he will never leave you nor forsake you. Do not be afraid; do not be discouraged."*

- God made it so you can have a baby. He knows all that goes into the process. So, allow Him to have His way from start to finish.

Week 38
PLEASE CONDITION MY PARTNER FOR OUR NEW BABY

Lord,

Please have your way in my partner's life. I know I will need all the help I can get, and I pray my partner is ready. Raising a baby is a big responsibility that I can not do alone. Please give my partner the knowledge, wisdom, and understanding to take care of our baby. I also pray that patience, an overflow of unconditional love, and grace will flow through my partner when caring for our baby, in Jesus's name, Amen.

Isaiah 40:5 NIV

> "And the glory of the LORD will be revealed, and all people will see it together. For the mouth of the LORD has spoken."

- Although you carried the baby alone for all these weeks, pray for your partner daily. They will need the same strength, encouragement, patience, etc., because it is not easy raising a child. You will need your time to recover. In the meantime, your partner will need your prayers.

Week 39
THANK YOU FOR THE BLESSING OF LIFE

Dear God,

I am so honored that you have chosen me to have this baby. The process was long and challenging, but not everyone was chosen for this. I can not wait to hold my baby in my arms for the first time. I feel as if we know each other already, and I can't wait to learn more. Thank you for blessing my womb and allowing me to carry one of your children, in Jesus's name, Amen.

Deuteronomy 28:4 NIV

> *"The fruit of your womb will be blessed, and the crops of your land and the young of your livestock—the calves of your herds and the lambs of your flocks."*

- Many think children are a burden because society forces you to focus on financial responsibility alone. Please understand children are a blessing from God. Some people go through great lengths to have one child but come up empty-handed. Count it all joy to have become a mother.

Week 40
SUCCESSFUL LABOR

Jesus,

I am a little nervous. I do not know what to expect because each delivery is different. I pray that my process is a success and that you take away the pain. Please strengthen me and heal me quickly after the baby is born. Lord, I pray my baby develops how it should also, in Jesus's name, Amen.

2 Thessalonians 3:16 NIV

> "Now may the Lord of peace himself give you peace at all times and in every way. The Lord be with all of you."

- God did not give us the spirit of fear. He gave us power, love, and a sound mind to get through life with ease. Give God your concern so you can walk in victory. I decree and declare your labor will be smooth.

www.ingramcontent.com/pod-product-compliance
Lightning Source LLC
Chambersburg PA
CBHW071424070526
44578CB00003B/680